Lunch boxes

A guide to healthy eating

Published by Happy Cat Books
An imprint of Catnip Publishing Ltd.
Islington Business Centre
3-5 Islington High Street
London N1 9LQ

This edition published 2006
1 3 5 7 9 10 8 6 4 2

A CIP catalogue record for this book is available from the British Library
ISBN 10: 1 905117 05 1
ISBN 13: 978-1-905117-05-5

Printed in China by WKT Co. Ltd.

Lunch boxes

A guide to healthy eating

Althea

Illustrated by Chris O'Neill

HAPPY CAT
BOOKS

These children are all enjoying a school lunch. The food in this picture will help to keep us healthy.

Some children choose to bring a packed lunch.
What have they brought today?

Food gives us energy and keeps us warm.
It also makes us grow and keeps us healthy.

Most foods that we like contain a mixture of the
things that do us good.

Steven has tuna fish sandwiches, a tomato, with yoghurt and an orange for afters.

The protein in tuna fish helps our bodies to grow properly and stay in good repair. If you fall over and cut yourself your body will use protein to make new skin. Meat, fish, eggs, cheese, nuts, beans and lentils all contain protein.

Anna believes that it is wrong to eat meat. We say she is a vegetarian. Her rice salad with beans and nuts gives her body-building protein. The beans and nuts also contain fibre. We need fibre to help us keep healthy and to stop us from getting constipated.

Fibre is in many fruits and vegetables as well as in wholemeal bread and some breakfast cereals. Her banana also contains fibre.

Ben brings a piece of cheese, a thick slice of bread, a tomato, carrots and an apple. His dad calls it a ploughman's lunch.

As well as protein, cheese contains calcium which we need for strong bones. The tomato and apple contain vitamin C and the carrot contains vitamin A. If we eat a mixed diet, we should get all the vitamins and minerals we need.

Justin has peanut butter sandwiches with jam – his favourite. His mum wouldn't let him bring a chocolate biscuit, because he's already had jam. She says eating sugary foods too often is bad for your teeth. Instead he has yoghurt and a tangerine.

He has to remember to take a pill at lunchtime, so he brings that in his lunch box too.

Kelly's mum has given her a grilled sausage, with rolls and lettuce.

Her mum says it is better to grill food when you can, as it's not good to eat too much fried food, and they had chips for supper last night.

To keep healthy, some people must always avoid certain foods.

Jemma has diabetes. She has to be careful about what and when she eats. Today she has chicken sandwiches with tomato and cucumber. She has also brought two satsumas and an apple. She had a digestive biscuit at breaktime.

Rashida's mum has made her meat and vegetable samosas. Rashida can't eat eggs or nuts, they make her very ill. She knows not to taste Justin's sandwiches. She even has to be careful not to touch the nuts on the bird table, in case she licks her fingers afterwards.

When she and her mum go shopping they read the labels carefully to make sure they don't buy food that might contain nuts. Even tiny amounts can make her very poorly. She has to be extra careful to ask before she eats anything at parties.

Tony has brought a thick slice of pizza, with cheese, ham and tomatoes on top. He has a packet of crisps and an orange. He's only allowed crisps once a week.

Kate has brought ham and salad sandwiches, yoghurt and a banana. She has a cereal bar in case she's still hungry.

A few months ago Kate was always tired. She didn't like getting up in the mornings, so she hardly had time for breakfast.

Mum was worried, she took Kate to the doctor. He said she was feeling tired because she missed breakfast and so she didn't get enough energy in the morning. Now she has cereal with milk – and toast and jam before she comes to school. She feels much better.

Class 3c are doing a topic on food. They have made some posters.

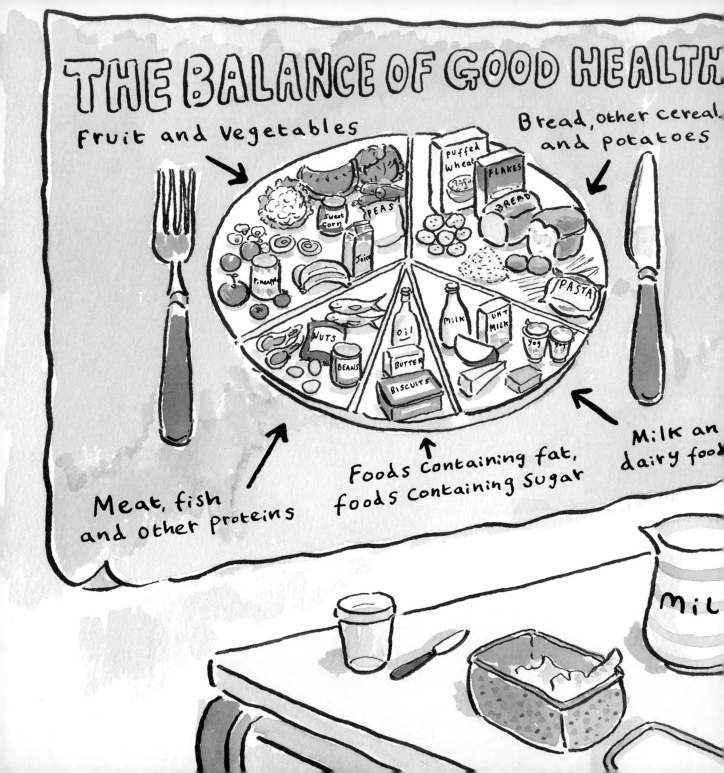

Healthy eating means having three meals a day, starting with breakfast, and eating a variety of different foods.

If you are using a lot of energy you may need an extra snack between meals. Jason has a glass of milk. Sam's mum gives him a pear and a scone.

Other titles by **Althea** *in the Talking it Through series*

Asthma
Be Careful
Dyslexia
Hospital
I Can't Hear Like You
When Uncle Bob Died